HOME SERIES

HOME SERIES
CONTEMPORARY KITCHENS

BETA-PLUS

CONTENTS

P. 4-5
A contemporary and highly colourful kitchen made by Wilfra.

P. 6
A kitchen with a timeless and classic style created and realized by Tack.

INTRODUCTION

O ver the course of the XXth century, the kitchen was undoubtedly the room that experienced the greatest changes, between technological innovations and the evolution of lifestyles. Today it holds an important place and is considered the beating heart of the home.

A need for space, a desire for exchanges, it naturally became a complete room to live in. The new generation of kitchens now welcomes the dining room without complex.

Convivial, open in all regards, today it is designed with the same aesthetic care as the reception rooms and is careful with its décor. Whether in a classic or design spirit, it is more sophisticated. Sometimes it shows itself off proudly, sometimes it conceals technical appliances and white goods to make it almost undetectable.

Raised to this chosen position, it transforms into a new concept, that of the kitchen living room: two spaces that nevertheless combine harmoniously.

But the open kitchen is already experiencing change: the bar trend is fading and increasingly making way for the central island or other solutions.

Each article presented in this work expresses a specific design of the art of living in today's kitchen. Discover a new place to live through pictures...

P. 8
A countryside kitchen realized with old materials, signed Vandemoortel.

P. 10-11
A kitchen for living in realized by Tack.

BLACK AND WHITE HARMONY

T his kitchen was realized by Wilfra ID&E, in partnership with the interior architecture agency Ensemble & Associés.

Experts in kitchen production for fifty-five years, Wilfra ID&E has expanded its range of activities since then to the global layout of residential and office projects, both in Belgium and abroad. The project presented here illustrates sharp mastery in the conception of a space: a geometry strongly linked to a functional and rational layout for an extremely spacious kitchen with an ultra-contemporary look.

The combination of white Silestone with black stained and deep sandblasted oak laminate gives architecture and structure to the kitchen.

Remember...

> Play with strong contrasts in colour and materials: black/white, wood/marble to create a refined effect.

> Shelving is placed along the wall to lighten the whole.

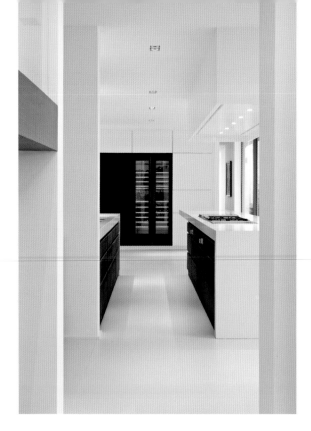

To limit the amount of materials used and to give the kitchen a serene spirit, the floors, work surfaces, wall coverings and shelves were realized in the same white Silestone.

The fully suspended work surface, that is used as a table, dominates the kitchen. The high wall of cupboards combines black oak laminate and white lacquer and matches the stone.

A NEW LOOK

AT A COUNTRYSIDE SPIRIT

F rank Tack has built up a solid reputation as a kitchen designer and creator for top of the range living, including in France (his company has been well-established in Paris for some months).

The kitchen shown in this article displays a timeless charm thanks to work realized in the chromatic range: refined and weathered colours dress the whole. A soft, soothing and extremely elegant ambiance.

These classic countryside kitchens breathe warmth and intimacy. Through the choice of natural top quality materials and the inclusion of all the elements in the project (colour, lighting, etc.) each realization is unique and well-thought through for the most demanding of clients.

Remember...

> Choose soft and neutral colours, beige, grey, taupe and especially ultra-mat paint for a cosy effect.
Nevertheless resistant and washable paints can be found with this mat effect generally reserved for the living rooms.

The robust Aga range has been sophisticatedly integrated in the global concept of this living kitchen.

TWO KITCHENS

IN A LUXURY PENTHOUSE

T he two kitchens in this article belong to an exceptional penthouse in many respects: a luxurious apartment on two stories with great allure and the surface area of the countryside residence (over 1 000 m^2), but offering a unique view of the sea…

The two projects emanate a holiday home ambiance and reveal luxury without ostentation. The choice of a specific lifestyle runs through these two kitchens: a desire for clarity, simplicity and functionality.

This kitchen was designed and released by Obumex.
In the dining corner, a Lloyd Loom table and JNL chairs.

Décor ideas

> Furniture without edges for pure lines and a very light graphic look.

> The wall covering takes up the furniture design to create a cosy ensemble.

> The stylish chest of drawers brings a touch of refinement and overturns a rather modern décor ...

The kitchen to welcome guests,
with wall cladding of painted MDF
and work surfaces in bluestone.
The oak floor has been whitened.
A project by Philip Simoen.

RESOLUTELY CONTEMPORARY

T he famous kitchen designer Frank Tack not only realizes timeless kitchens with a typical countryside style (see p. 20-25): he also creates resolutely contemporary kitchens.

The kitchen for living presented in this article is an illustration of this. A sober design and pure lines, while still emanating a certain warmth thanks to the colours chosen and the presence of natural wood panelling.

This minimalist project appears like a striking, discrete and timeless stylish figure.

The worked wood is combined with a finish with brushed bands: proof that minimalist kitchens are not necessarily cold…

Décor ideas

> Kitchen furniture with different finishes: natural wood and grey paint to break the monotony and differentiate between the volumes.

> The suspended ceiling, holds both the spots and the extractor fan: a top of the range system.

CONFRONTATION

OF ROUGH AND ELEGANT

T his spacious apartment on the Belgian coast offering magnificent views of the sea was revisited by the interior architects from 'aksent.

The materials and colours were chosen in cooperation with Matthijs & Co.

The discrete atmosphere ensures that the apartment is not limited to being a summer residence: it is wonderful to stay here at any time of year.

A kitchen that is both simple and elegant.

The elegance and refinement of the armchairs in beautiful velvet and leather and a small ebony and bronze table (Promemoria collection) contrast with the roughness of the floor (sawn oak floorboads). Sophisticated shades in silk.
The small format dark brown marble stands out against the rough character of the kitchen floorboards. Shagreen covers the chairs, custom-made by Promemoria, combines with a Varenna table (Promemoria – Collezione Sozzi). A bronze and silk lamp from the same collection completes the ensemble. The kitchen was realised in rough treated pine.

Décor ideas

> The credence in aesthetic and practical glass to protect the walls discretely. Reflections from the glass give refinement and depth.

> The juxtaposition of rough elements with other more contemporary: a contemporary black table on a floor of worn ardoise marble, glass credence addressing the furniture in the panelling.

A SECULAR PATINA

A ndreas Van Apers has built up a solid reputation over a few decades as a wholesaler in used construction materials and architectural antiquities.

His son Joris is continuing the tradition in his own company, while adding an important dimension to his father's work: he designs and also realises complete interior decoration…

This kitchen, realised from A to Z by Joris Van Apers, bathes in an XVIIIth century atmosphere.

Old flagstones from Bourgogne were chosen for the floor arranged in a free pattern.

Remember

> Transoms above the doors such as visual piercing allow the light to circulate and lighten the construction.

> All the modern electrical appliances are concealed: nothing should break the spirit of the space.

P. 45-51
Using original elements, appropriate ageing techniques and respect for the proportions made it possible to recreate the atmosphere of a genuine XVIIIth century kitchen.

The cooking area includes an extractor hood built-into a XVIIIth century fireplace, a work surface surrounding the centre in coloured polished concrete and hand-made small grey anthracite doors.

A MULTIFUNCTIONAL KITCHEN

OPEN TO NATURE

T he kitchen of this countryside home was bespoke designed by the architect Annik Dierckx.

It relates to a global concept that easily adapts to the various stages of the life of the owners: from a young active family to the less-able retired couple.

Both the exterior and interior architecture have been cared for to the tiniest detail so that all the elements are in harmony with each other. The result: a serene, harmonious and balanced whole that breathes calm and serenity.

Throughout this home – and a fortiori in the kitchen – the marriage of the classical elements is assisted with contemporary aesthetics.

The kitchen for living in was in the wooden barn adjacent to a brick wall of the main part of the house. The kitchen area extends visually towards the terrace thanks to the large glazed partition that opens up onto the garden. The open fire, at kitchen table height, gives the whole a warm and convivial touch.

Remember...

> The contrast between the traditional oak beams and the sober and contemporary look of the white kitchen give the whole a surprising and timeless character.

> The varnished elements, furniture and glass credence, a strong trend in contemporary kitchens: they give a touch of sophistication.

HARMONY

OF MATERIALS AND COLOURS

T he interior architect Linda Coart and the architect firm Schellen designed the entirety of this open plan kitchen annex/dining room.

Materials and colours merge in perfect harmony.

The living room, the central dining area and the kitchen adjoin each other without truly being separated. The visual contact between the occupants is omnipresent, the view over the garden unrestricted.

Two ovens and an espresso machine give a special touch to the wooden wall in the kitchen.
A part of the wall – in extension – provided with panelling is in fact a door that gives access to the basement and a storage room.

Remember

> The furniture in walnut coloured wood, an increasingly popular shade.

> A chic, rational and elegant kitchen thanks to the discretion of the full height furniture and the built in electrical appliances.

SYNERGY

OF NEW AND OLD

T he private loft of the architect Pieter Vandenhout reveals an assertive temperament.

Rough materials like grey concrete cover the walls and floors creating an ultra-design and minimalist envelope.

Only the red credence revives this sober interior.

The kitchen is situated in an alcove and has a restricted place in this vast space.

An industrial spirit mixed with rustic notes, a daring but successful alliance.

Rough and hard materials (polished concrete, stainless steel, …) merge with bright shades.

Remember

> The part in grey is created and produced on different materials: concrete, stainless steel and wood, for an original and mysterious look.

> The contrast created by the long rustic oak table: an, almost theatrical, strong staging.

A DESIRE

FOR FLUIDITY AND PURITY

R estructured by the interior architect Anne Derasse, this apartment situated in Saint-Germain-des-Prés in a typically Haussmann building displays a desire for fluidity and purity.

A contemporary look for the kitchen thanks to stainless steel and the pure design of the furniture mixed with a cosy spirit realised through the omnipresence of wood. The Haussman characteristics of this room have disappeared in favour of a suspended ceiling equipped with multiple spotlights.

The dining room itself preserved its classic mouldings. The room nevertheless looks contemporary, notably thanks to the graphic openings in the corridor.

The kitchen is realised in oak with a stainless steel work surface and credence. The high furniture and electrical appliances are concealed behind panels that reach from floor to ceiling and with mat enamel. The table is framed under shelves used for storing the contemporary Limoges Porcelain tableware; the chairs are wicker. Paintings of earthenware from Morocco hang on the wall.

Décor ideas

> The parquet kept in the kitchen. If vitrified it can withstand water or grease stains without any problem and it makes the room warmer.

> The stainless steel credence: easy to install and it protects the wall and gives a contemporary look.

> The highly designed ultra-fine work surface.

Above the chimney, an Indian window with ornamental apertures from the XVIth century. Louis XVI chairs covered in weathered patina leather, with the Chartier stamp.
A large oval Louis XVI table with six multifaceted feet on castors.

A PASSION

FOR OLD WOOD

O ver the years, Corvelyn has brought together a precious and singular stock of old wooden floors: a Parisian oak flooring from the XVIIIth century, old floorboards of American pitch pine 12 m long and 30 cm wide, old wicker racks 4 m long and 30 cm wide, old teak floorboards from Bali, ...

In this second kitchen realised by him, according to a project by the architect Bernard De Clerck, Corvelyn shows a sample of the creativity he has proven through witnessing to a past long-gone...

Result: an authentic kitchen.

The patina of these old floorboards is authentic: They acquired this weathered look over the course of the centuries.

Old pine wooden boards originally from a warehouse in Nancy were integrated in this kitchen. With a conical form they have a width of 50 cm: the craftsman of the age wanted to use the widest possible boards.

Décor idea

> Juxtapose opposites: an extremely fine and pure suspended glass contrasts with the rustic elements in the room.

The high doors of the cupboard discretely house all the kitchen utensils
The floor is laid with old bluestone flagstones.

AN ULTRA-CONTEMPORARY

CHATEAU KITCHEN

The historic chateau of Ommerstein was restored in depth by the team at the project firm Simoni, in cooperation with Scoop.

The chateau was transformed on numerous occasions over the course of the years. The roof was in a disastrous state and the interior was distressingly banal. For this reason the decision was taken to dismantle the chateau and to start the renovation process practically from zero. The principal wanted to furnish the chateau luxuriously. For that reason the choice was made for a modern design always mixed with a certain amount of classic style.

The kitchen is resolutely contemporary and extremely elegant. The work surfaces in natural stone were realised by Van den Weghe (The Stonecompany). The floors, walls and central island were covered in Pietra Piasentina.

Remember...

> The subtle marriage of sober and neutral colours and the mat/gloss contrast. The walls give refinement but also softness as they are covered with mat paint. This mat nature confronted with the glossy floor and work surface offers timeless elegance.

A KITCHEN

IN THE OLD STABLES

T his superb farm is one of the exceptional realisations of the architect Raymond Rombouts. Characterised by its long façade, it was recently renovated by the interior architect Alexis Herbosch (Apluz).

Alexis Herbosch and the client were careful to preserve the harmony between the existing building and the annexe. The alliance between the proportions and the materials used guaranteed the complementariness of the whole. Almost as though the annexe building had always been there…

The kitchen was reconstructed in the stables. To recreate the original atmosphere of the rear façade, the two existing windows were replaced by a new oak door. The floor was laid with large old tambour weathered flagstones.

Remember...

> Unmatched chairs repainted in pastel shades modernise the whole.

The glazed cupboard in sombre – almost "battleship grey" – colour breaks the white purity of the dining room.

P. 88-89
The small metal window in the wall of
the black zelliges located behind the
cooker allows the chef to see the guests
arriving through the garden.

A LIVING KITCHEN

FOR A FUTURIST

I n an extremely coveted district, Olivier Michel, the founder of Upptown, discovered a number of abandoned warehouses and garages that were quickly transformed into a residential project comprising four ultramodern lofts.

The original intention was to sell these four lofts but Michel and his wife became so passionate for the project that they decided to merge two units to create an extremely large plot. In fact it offers over 600 m² of habitable area supplemented by its own garden, a swimming pool and two indoor patios. The construction was entrusted to the architect Bruno Corbisier.

The Upptown team realised the entire interior layout.

The stainless steel work surface of this futuristic kitchen is part of the Boffi collection. The four metre long table was realised in Corian marble. The transparent bar stools are from Kartell. Streaked wallpaper from Eijffinger and a black sofa from Ipe Cavalli.
The kitchen wall is covered with white enamelled plates of plaster with an undulating effect from ModularArts.

Décor ideas

> The transparent barstools do not impede the space and emphasise the pure ambient spirit.

> The immaculate whiteness: a decorative element that is always a success.

A KITCHEN WITH A VIEW

OVER LAKE GENEVA

This 300 m² apartment situated in Geneva with a wonderful view over Lake Geneva was completely rethought and rearranged by the interior architects John-Paul Welton and Brigitte Boiron, moving from the classical to a highly sophisticated timeless modernity.

The new apartment in the Haussman style has become a jewel of originality and contemporary design. It plays with the contrast between black and white, the combinations of materials and exceptional luminosity to offer brightly coloured artworks a select place.

They created an additional bathroom and changed the kitchen. The apartment was entirely repainted white: originally it was decorated in a very classical and coloured style. The original oak-stained parquet was stained wenge.

The kitchen is entered by a sliding glass door.
For this kitchen Arclinea "Kitchen Ambiance", the electrical appliances from Siemens were chosen.
The floor is made from polished concrete. Curtains from No Limit.

The dining room with the white varnished Marilyn table with a central chrome foot bespoke production from Welton Design. Brigitta chairs from Promemoria. The large light (180 cm diameter) is from VG Newtrend (resin Globe). Photograph of Madonna by Claudio Moser.
To the left of the large photograph, a lithograph by the painter Soulage.
Sculpture in bronze Maternité by Jeff Troll. Padded armchair in white leather and chrome by Mies van der Rohe. A coloured cow sculpture by David Gerstein.

Remember...

> The combination of classicism of the original interior architecture and ultra-design furniture. Moulding, parquets make the ultramodern furniture warmer.

> The maxi-suspension visually restricts the dining room.

FREEDOM AND SPACE

T his project by the architect Hans Verstuyft includes a complex private residential programme combined with professional activities.

The two fields are clearly separated in any event.

The structure had to fulfil the laws of division: a freer plan was consequently required.

The division of the space is entirely free thanks to the assembly of the concrete slab column.

The modularity of the façades is strictly limited to 90 cm or to a multiple of this width.

A window or a wall may be positioned where it proves necessary. Each interior or exterior space may thereby be optimised to the extreme.

The work surface, table and chairs were bespoke design to offer space warmth and functionality.

The kitchen-dining room emanates the same feeling of warmth.
The exterior room and its open fire perfectly complement the kitchen.

Décor ideas

> A wall divided in two horizontally: the furniture stained black on the lower section contrast with the finesse of the shelves and the whiteness of the walls on the upper section.
A layout that breaks with the traditional layout of kitchens often equipped with high wall units.

A TIMELESS AMBIANCE

T his timeless kitchen annexe and dining room was realised from A to Z by Joris Van Apers with old materials from the family company Andreas Van Apers.

Use of original elements, the appropriate weathering techniques and respect for proportions made it possible to recreate the atmosphere of a timeless kitchen, reminiscent of the century preferred by Joris Van Apers, the XVIIIth...

The work surface, table and chairs were bespoke designed to offer space, warmth and functionality.

An old sink hand made in Carrere marble. A Lacanche range. The wall is covered in small white Dutch tiles.

View of the kitchen for living. Hexagonal floor tiles in white-beige terracotta in an irregular pattern.

On the floor, large flagstones of
old white Carrere marble.
A true XVIIIth ambiance.

Remember...

> A timeless cachet. The patina of the
walls echoes other old elements: floors,
tiling and an array of copper pans; no
intrusion breaks the general ambiance.

A COUNTRYSIDE KITCHEN

WITH A CHATEAU ALLURE

T his imposing country estate situated in the region of Lille has both the charm of a countryside home and the allure of a chateau. The majestic volumes of this building of over 1 000 m^2 were built in 1920 according to plans by Charles Bourgeois. The finish is the most luxurious: doors and frames in solid oak, marble floors and chimneys, exclusive parquets, etc.

The owner, a famous designer and producer of films, has shown her creative talent in this unique staging. She restored the original single-family cachet of this mansion, which had been divided into a dozen apartments over the years.

P. 110-115
The kitchen, equipped by a double La Cornue stove, is on the street side. The recovered tiles from Van Den Bogaert. Leon were combined with floorboards covered with weathered patina from Antiekbouw.

Remember...

> A kitchen out of the ordinary is a studied setting: the extraordinary La Cornue stove is the star of the piece and is treated as such: no high element will over-stage its presence.

HOME SERIES

Volume 19 : CONTEMPORARY KITCHENS

The reports in this book are selected from the Beta-Plus collection of home-design books: www.betaplus.com
They have been compiled in a special series by Le Figaro in French language: Ma Déco

Copyright © 2009 Beta-Plus Publishing / Le Figaro
Originally published in French language

PUBLISHER
Beta-Plus Publishing
Termuninck 3
B – 7850 Enghien
Belgium
www.betaplus.com
info@betaplus.com

TEXT
Alexandra Druesne

PHOTOGRAPHY
Jo Pauwels

DESIGN
Polydem - Nathalie Binart

TRANSLATIONS
Txt-Ibis

ISBN: 978-90-8944-050-1

Printed in China